THIS COPY OF SANTA'S CHRISTMAS JOKE BOOK

BELONGS TO

Also in Beaver by Katie Wales
THE ELEPHANT JOKE BOOK
JOKES FROM OUTER SPACE

and by Katie Wales with David McKee
A BOOK OF ELEPHANTS

SANTA'S CHRISTMAS JOKE BOOK

KATIE WALES

Illustrated by Kevin Smith

Beaver Books

A Happy
Christmas to everyone, especially Tim

A Beaver Book
Published by Arrow Books Limited
62-65 Chandos Place, London WC2N 4NW
An imprint of Century Hutchinson Limited

London Melbourne Sydney Auckland
Johannesburg and agencies throughout
the world

First published 1986
Reprinted 1986 and 1987

Text © Katie Wales 1986
Illustrations © Century Hutchinson Ltd 1986

Set in Linotron Century Schoolbook
by Input Typesetting Ltd, London SW19 8DR

Printed and bound in Great Britain by
Anchor Brendon Limited, Tiptree, Essex

ISBN 0 09 950550 9

Contents

Santa's Christmas Greetings

Knock, knock.
Who's there?
Mary.
Mary who?
Mary Christmas everybody!

What did one angel say to the other angel?
'Halo there!'

What is Tarzan's favourite Christmas song?
Jungle bells.

How do cats greet each other at Christmas?
'A furry merry Christmas and a Happy Mew Year.'

What do elephants sing at Christmas?
'No-elephants, No-elephants . . .'

What does Dracula write on his Christmas cards?
'Best vicious of the season.'

What do angry mice send each other at Christmas?
Cross-mouse cards.

What do monsters sing at Christmas?
'Deck the halls with poison ivy,
Tra-lalala-la . . . '

What is Dracula's favourite Christmas song?
'I'm dreaming of a fright Christmas.'

What did one Christmas candle ask the other?
'Going out tonight?'

What did one Christmas bell say to another?
'Give me a ring sometime.'

What Christmas carol is popular in the desert?
O camel ye faithful.

Knock, knock.
Who's there?
Yule.
Yule who?
Yule never walk alone . . .

Knock, knock.
Who's there?
Wendy.
Wendy who?
*Wendy red, red robin comes bob, bob, bobbin'
along.*

How do sheep greet each other at Christmas?
'A merry Christmas to ewe.'

What does Santa Claus write on his Christmas cards?
ABCDEFGHIJKMNOPQRSTUVWXYZ (No L – geddit?)

Knock, knock.
Who's there?
Ivy.
Ivy who?
Ivy long to Glasgow . . .

Knock, knock.
Who's there?
Snow.
Snow who?
Snow business like show business . . .

Knock, knock.
Who's there?
Wenceslas
Wenceslas who?
Wenceslas train home?

Knock, knock.
Who's there?
Dexter.
Dexter who?
Dexter hall with boughs of holly . . .

Knock, knock.
Who's there?
Wayne.
Wayne who?
Wayne in a manger . . .

Knock, knock.
Who's there?
Doughnut.
Doughnut who?
Doughnut open till Christmas.

Knock, knock.
Who's there?
Oakham
Oakham who?
Oakham all ye faithful . . .

Knock, knock
Who's there?
Rudolph.
Rudolph who?
Money is the Rudolph all evil.

Knock, knock.
Who's there?
Avery.
Avery who?
Avery merry Christmas.

Knock, knock.
Who's there?
Holly.
Holly who?
Hollydays are here again . . .

Knock, knock.
Who's there?
Igloo.
Igloo who?
Igloo knew Susie like I know Susie . . .

Santa's Grotto

What is Santa's wife called?
Mary Christmas.

How do you know Santa likes gardening?
Because he shouts 'Hoe, hoe.'

What's green and cries 'ho, ho'?
Santa Pickle.

Why is a lion in the desert like Father
Christmas?
Because of its Sandy Claws.

Who claps at Christmas time?
Santapplause.

What is written on Rudolph's stable?
'Santa rules, but deers rei(g)n.'

What is written on the back of Santa's sleigh?
'My other sleigh's a Porsche.'

Where does a drunken Father Christmas live?
The Fairy Blotto.

How does Jack Frost get to work?
By icicle.

What goes 'ho, swish, ho, swish'?
Santa caught in a revolving door.

What exams did Santa Claus take?
Ho, ho, ho levels.

What goes 'ho, ho, ho, bonk'?
Santa Claus laughing his head off.

What do you get if you cross a cocoa bean with
a deer?
Chocolate moose.

Why doesn't St Nicholas shave?
Every time he tries, he nicks himself.

Where do fairies do their Christmas shopping?
British Gnome Stores.

What did Santa's wife say when he asked what
the noise was on the roof?
'It's the rain (rein) dear (deer).'

What has antlers and eats cheese?
Mickey Moose.

What would happen if Minnehaha married
Santa Claus?
She'd become Minnehoho.

What is the wettest animal?
A reindeer.

Why does Santa wear red trousers?
Because his blue ones are at the cleaners.

Why does Santa wear red braces?
To hold his trousers up.

Where do the fairies go to recover after
working so hard at Christmas?
Elf farms.

Did you hear the joke about the two deer?
You didn't? Dear, dear . . .

What do you call a deer with one eye?
No idea . . .

What do you give a deer with indigestion?
Elka-selzer.

PATIENT: Doctor, doctor, I feel like Father
Christmas.
DOCTOR: Well open your mouth and say "Ho,
ho".

What do you get if you cross Father Christmas
with Sherlock Holmes?
Santa Clues.

Santa at the North Pole

What nationality is Santa?
North Polish.

What is a fjord?
A Norwegian car.

Where do Eskimos get their milk from?
Eskimoos.

Why do Eskimos eat whale meat and blubber?
You would too, if you had to eat whale meat all the time!

What's the difference between the North Pole and the South Pole?
All the difference in the world.

What do polar bears eat for a snack?
Ice bergers.

Why do polar bears have fur coats?
They'd look silly in anoraks.

How do you make a Mexican chilli?
Take him to the North Pole.

What is brown with a hump, and is found at
the North Pole?
A lost camel.

What's furry and minty?
A polo bear.

What do you get if you cross a polar bear with
a kangaroo?
A fur coat with very large pockets.

What do you call an Eskimo's house without a toilet?
An Ig.

What is a polar bear's favourite biscuit?
A Penguin. (Yes, I *know* penguins live at the *South* Pole . . .)

What's black and white and goes round and round?
A penguin in a revolving door.

What kind of warmth do sheep enjoy in the Arctic Circle?
Central bleating.

What's white and goes up?
A silly snowflake.

Where do snowmen dance?
At a snowball.

What do Eskimos buy their Christmas
presents with?
Ice lolly.

What's black and white and red all over?
A sunburnt penguin.

What goes out black and comes back white?
A black cow in a snowstorm.

Why do Eskimos eat candles?
For light refreshment.

Why is it difficult to keep a secret at the North
Pole?
Because your teeth keep chattering.

How do Eskimos dress?
As quickly as possible.

What do you get if you cross a hush puppy
with ice?
A slush puppy.

What do you call someone whose mother was
born in the Arctic Circle and whose father
was born in Cuba?
An ice cube.

Did you hear about the baby polar bear who
kept asking his mum and dad and aunts and
uncles if he was 100 per cent pure polar bear?
'Why do you ask?' they all said.
'Well,' he replied. 'I'm flipping *freezing*!!'

What's big and icy and tastes delicious?
A glacier mint.

Why do birds fly south in winter?
Because it's too far to walk.

What kind of ball is fun but doesn't bounce?
A snowball.

What's black and white and blue all over?
A zebra at the North Pole.

How do you send a message to a Viking?
By Norse code.

What do monsters like best about the North Pole?
Slay-riding.

What do you get if you cross a snowman with a shark?
Frost bite.

Did you hear the joke about the snowman?
It would leave you cold.

29

What happens when you slip on thin ice?
Your bottom gets thaw.

What did the polar bear take on holiday?
Just the bear essentials.

How does an Eskimo build a house?
Igloos it together.

What is a mushroom?
A place where Eskimos train huskies.

A very successful central-heating salesman
sold his wares even in the Arctic Circle. One
day an Eskimo complained that when he'd
taken his stove with him on a fishing trip his
canoe had caught fire.
'Well,' said the salesman. 'You can't have your
kayak and heat it.'

When is a boat like a heap of snow?
When it's adrift.

What's big, white and furry, and found in Birmingham?
A polar bear that's lost.

Why did the little girl bury her father in the snow?
Because she liked cold pop.

How do you make anti-freeze?
Send her to the North Pole.

What is ploughed but never planted?
Snow.

What trees are always sad?
Pine trees.

What trees are always warm?
Fir (fur) trees.

What do you get if you cross an alligator with an iceberg?
A cold snap.

What's an executioner's favourite sport?
Sleighing.

Where do you find the most fish?
Finland.

What do you get if you cross a witch with an iceberg?
A cold spell.

What is a cold war?
A snowball fight.

What do you need to spot a polar bear half a mile away?
Good ice-sight.

What water won't freeze?
Boiling water.

What wears a coat all winter and pants all summer?
A dog.

Knock, knock.
Who's there?
Martini.
Martini who?
Martini hands are frozen.

What is the hardest thing about learning to skate?
The ice.

What's a Laplander?
A clumsy man on a bus.

What's the difference between an iceberg and a clothes brush?
One crushes boats and the other brushes coats.

What do you call an Eskimo in ear-muffs?
Anything you like, he can't hear you.

What's black and white and noisy?
A penguin who got a drumkit for Christmas.

What message hangs above an Eskimo's mantelpiece?
'Snow place like home.'

What's black and white and bounces?
A penguin on a pogo-stick.

What's black and white and has eight wheels?
A penguin on roller skates.

Did you hear about the miser at the North Pole?
He sat by a candle to keep warm. I didn't say he lit it ...

Why shouldn't you tell a joke while you're ice-skating?
The ice might crack up.

How did the Eskimo girl get rid of her boyfriend?
She gave him the cold shoulder.

What sort of athlete would be warmest at the North Pole?
A long jumper.

What travels faster – heat or cold?
Heat: it's easy to catch cold.

What do you call a smelly polar bear?
Winnie the Pooh.

How does a polar bear enjoy the Christmas spirit?
On the rocks.

What is the coldest country in the world?
Chile.

How can you spell chilly using just two letters?
I.C.

What is ice?
Skid stuff.

Santa's Christmas Eve

What did Adam say on the day before Christmas?
'It's Christmas, Eve.'

How do you make a Wally laugh on Boxing Day?
Tell him a joke on Christmas Eve.

What do you have in December that you don't have in any other month?
The letter 'D'.

Did you hear about the little boy who was given an unbreakable, shockproof, waterproof, anti-magnetic watch for Christmas?
He lost it.

What does Father Christmas suffer from if he gets stuck in the chimney?
Santa claustrophobia.

What do you call a letter that is sent up the chimney at Christmas?
Blackmail.

Who delivers cats' Christmas presents?
Santa Paws.

What's the best Christmas present?
It's hard to say, but a drum takes a lot of beating . . .

What is the difference between children at Christmas and werewolves?
Werewolves have claws on their fingers; children have Claus on their minds.

Why does Santa Claus go down the chimney?
Because it soots him.

Did you hear about the dad who was so mean
that he went out of the house on Christmas
Eve, fired his air-gun, and came back and said
Santa Claus was dead?

Who delivers elephants' Christmas presents?
Elephanta Claus.

What's the worst thing to get for Christmas?
Measles.

What books did Dracula get for Christmas?
Ghouliver's Travels and *Mother Ghost's
Nursery Rhymes.*

Who gets the sack on Christmas Eve?
Santa Claus.

Why did the boy's mother knit him three socks
for Christmas?
Because he'd grown another foot.

What did the miser give his wife for
Christmas?
A ladder in her stocking.

Who brings Dracula's Christmas presents?
Santa Claws.

Where is the best place to buy a Christmas present for your dog?
Leeds.

Where is the best place to buy a present for your cat?
Fishguard.

Where does the Queen do her Christmas shopping?
Newcastle.

Where does a plumber do his Christmas shopping?
Bath.

What did the octopus get for Christmas?
Four pairs of gloves.

Where does Noddy do his Christmas shopping?
Redcar.

Where does a gardener do his Christmas
shopping?
Barrow (or Leek).

How many chimneys does Santa go down?
Stacks.

'The best Christmas present I ever received was a trumpet.'
'Why?'

'My father still gives me 50p a week not to blow it.'

Did you hear about the miser who gave his wife a gun and trap for Christmas?
She'd said she wanted a mink coat...

What did the little girl say when she got a violin for Christmas?
'Oh, fiddle.'

What did the witch get for Christmas?
A witch watch.

Why is Santa like a bear on Christmas Eve?
Because he's Sooty.

What's black and white and red all over?
Santa falling down a chimney.

Santa's Christmas Dinner

On what nuts can pictures hang?
Walnuts.

What beats his chest and swings from
Christmas cake to Christmas cake?
Tarzipan.

'Mum, can I have a dog for Christmas?
'No, you can have turkey like everyone else.'

What did the Eskimos sing when they got
their Christmas dinner?
*'Whalemeat again, don't know where, don't
know when...'*

What do you get if you cross egg-white with
gunpowder?
Boom-meringue.

What did the big cracker say to the little cracker?
'My pop's bigger than yours.'

Who is never hungry at Christmas?
The turkey – he's always stuffed.

What bird has wings but cannot fly?
Roast turkey.

What are the best things to put in a Christmas cake?
Your teeth.

Where is the best place to go for Christmas dinner?
Turkey.

What do you call a crate of ducks?
A box of quackers.

Why did they let the turkey join the band?
Because it had the drumsticks.

What do ghosts put on their turkey at Christmas?
Grave-y.

Why did the turkey cross the road?
To prove that he wasn't chicken.

What happens if you eat the Christmas decorations?
You get tinsel-itis.

Who was the trifle's favourite artist?
Bottijelli.

What did the mother turkey say to the baby turkey?
'If your father could see you now, he'd turn in his gravy.'

What do you call a baby turkey?
A goblet.

What do you take out of a frozen chicken's tummy?
The blizzard.

What's white and fluffy and beats his chest on the Christmas table?
A meringue-utang.

What's tall and wobbly and is found in Paris?
The Trifle Tower.

What is James Bond's favourite Christmas dish?
Min-spies.

What international disasters might happen if you dropped the Christmas dinner?
The downfall of Turkey, the disintegration of China, and the overthrow of Greece.

What do you get if you cross a football team
with ice-cream?
Aston vanilla.

What do you get if you cross a chicken with a
Christmas whisky?
Scotch eggs.

What do you get if you cross a turkey with an
octopus?
*I don't know what it's called, but everyone gets
a leg each.*

'We had Grandma for Christmas dinner.'
'Really? We had turkey.'

What do frogs like to drink?
Croaka cola.

What do frogs like to eat?
Lollihops.

What do monsters like for Christmas dinner?
Salimey sandwiches, and demonade.

What else?
Ghoulash.

What does Dracula like for his dessert?
Nectarines.

What else?
Leeches and scream.

What do ghosts eat for Christmas dinner?
Spook-etti.

How do fairies make their Christmas cake?
With elf-raising flour.

What do you get if you cross a sheep-dog with jelly?
Collie-wobbles.

Did you hear the about the idiot who stuffed jelly in his ears?
You might say he was a trifle deaf...

What do cannibals eat for Christmas dinner?
Baked beings.

Santa at the Pantomime

Why was Cinderella such a poor football
player?
She had a pumpkin for a coach.

What is beautiful, grey and wears glass
slippers?
Cinderellephant.

What is the scariest pantomine?
Ghouldilocks and the Three Bears.

Did you hear about the time when Ali Baba
stood outside the entrance to the cave and
commanded 'Open Sesame'?
From inside a voice cried 'Opens says-a-who?'

What pantomime is set in a chemist's shop?
Puss in Boots.

On which side of the house did Jack's
beanstalk grow?
On the outside.

Who looked after Finderella?
Her Fairy Codmother.

What is the ghosts' favourite Christmas
entertainment?
The phantomime.

What did Cinderella say when the chemist's
lost her photos?
'Some day my prints will come.'

What did one flea on Robinson Crusoe say to
the other?
'Bye for now – see you on Friday.'

Why did the farmer call his cockerel
Robinson?
Because he crew so.

Why was Cinderella kicked out of the netball team?
She kept running away from the ball.

What kind of pet did Aladdin have?
A flying car-pet.

Who invented the five-day week?
Robinson Crusoe: he had all his work done by Friday.

Who sailed the seven seas looking for rubbish and blubber?
Binbag the Whaler.

What did Little John say when Robin Hood accidentally shot him?
'That was an arrow escape.'

Did you hear about the actor who was so keen to get the part of Long John Silver that he had his leg cut off?
He still didn't get the job – it was the wrong leg.

Which member of Robin Hood's band was Welsh?
Rhyl Scarlet.

Why did Robin Hood steal money from the rich?
Because the poor didn't have any.

What is Snow White's favourite food?
Egg White. (Do you get the yolk?)

Knock, knock.
Who's there?
Aladdin.
Aladdin who?
Aladdin the street is waiting for you.

What gives milk, goes 'moo', and makes all your dreams come true?
Your Dairy Godmother.

Who wears a crown, lives in a delicatessen, and calls for his fiddlers three?
Old King Cole Slaw.

Who shouted 'knickers' at the big, bad wolf?
Little Rude Riding Hood.

Which pantomimes are the cheapest to see at Christmas?
Goldilocks and the One and a Half Bears, Snow White and the Three Dwarfs; Robin Hood and his Merry Man; and Jack and the Beanseed.

What do you get if you cross Humpty Dumpty with Mother Goose?
Either an egg-stra special pantomime, or an omelette.

Who in Treasure Island has a parrot that cries
'pieces of four'?
Short John Silver.

LONG JOHN
SILVER
AUDITIONS

Santa at the Circus

What is the difference between a barber in Rome and a mad circus owner?
One is a shaving Roman and the other is a raving showman.

Why did the tightrope walker ask for his bankbook?
In order to check his balance.

What did they call the lion tamer who put his right arm down the lion's throat?
Lefty.

Who are safe when a man-eating lion escapes from the circus?
Women and children.

Why did Nellie the elephant leave the circus?
She was tired of working for peanuts.

How did the human cannonball lose his job?
He got fired.

What is the last thing a trapeze artist wants
to be?
A fall guy.

What do you do with a blue elephant?
Take him to the circus to cheer him up.

When are circus acrobats needed at parties?
When tumblers are wanted.

Why is a circus a sad place?
Because the seats are in tiers.

Did you hear that Pinocchio was wanted for a job in the circus?
They had to pull a few strings. . .

Why is an alcoholic like a poor juggler?
They're both full of boos.

What's brown and funny and has a red nose?
Cocoa the Clown.

What is big, grey and too dangerous to appear in a circus?
An elephant with a machine-gun.

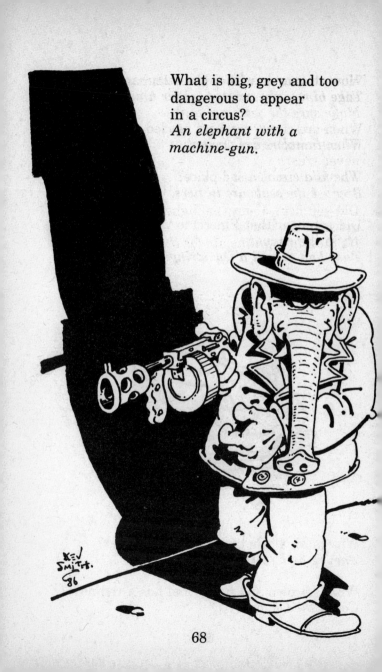

How do you make a circus audience sit on the edge of their seats?
Make sure the seats are high.

Which members of the circus band can you never trust?
The fiddlers.

Did you hear about the highest paid trapeze artist in the world?
He flies through the air for the greatest of fees.

Santa's Party Fun

What did the guests sing at the Eskimo's
Christmas party?
'Freeze a jolly good fellow. . .'

What do you get if you cross a conjurer with
a baby?
Bawl Daniels.

What party game did Jekyll like best?
Hyde and Seek.

Did you hear about the man who went to a
New Year's Eve party dressed as a bone?
A dog ate him in the hall.

What ballet is most popular with monsters?
Swamp Lake.

What would you do if you saw Dracula,
Frankenstein's monster, and the Incredible
Hulk?
Hope they were going to a fancy dress party.

Why couldn't the butterfly go to the ball?
Because it was a moth ball.

What is the difference between a ballerina and
a duck?
One dances Swan Lake, the other swims in it.

When is it dangerous to play cards?
When the joker is wild.

What do you get if you cross a small horn with
a little flute?
A tootie flooty.

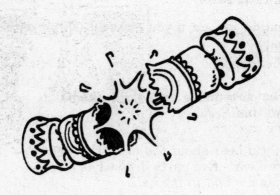

What is a frog's favourite game?
Croquet.

What is a crocodile's favourite game?
Snap.

What is a kangaroo's favourite game?
Hop-scotch.

What is a mouse's favourite game?
Hide and squeak.

What makes a chess player happy?
Taking a (k)night off.

Did you hear the joke about the poker game?
Never mind – it's no big deal.

Where do fortune tellers dance?
At the crystal ball.

How do chickens dance?
Chick to chick.

What is a dance for
buns?
Abundance.

What is a dance for
two tins?
The can-can.

Where do astronauts kiss at Christmas?
Under the missile-toe.

What did the balloon say to the pin?
'Hi, buster!'

What is the horse's favourite game?
Stable tennis.

How do you start a chicken race?
From scratch.

How do you start a pudding race?
Sago.

How do you start a flea race?
One, two, flea, go.

How do you start a teddy bear race?
Shout: Ready, teddy, go.

How do you start a jelly race?
Shout: Get Set.

What is a miser's favourite game?
Meanopoly.

What is a miserable person's favourite game?
Moanopoly.

What is a coal-
miner's favourite
game?
Mineopoly.

Knock, knock
Who's there?
Rupert.
Rupert who?
*Rupert your left hand in, rupert your left hand
out...*

What dance do hippies hate?
A *square dance.*

What TV game is most popular with fish?
Name that tuna.

What game do cannibals play at parties?
Swallow my leader.

What dance do ducks prefer?
The quackstep.

What is Dracula's favourite dance?
The vaults (waltz).

Where do they go dancing in California?
San Frandisco.

Where do geologists go for fun?
Rock concerts.

Why was the cricketer unhappy on New Year's Eve?
Because he missed the ball.

What game do ghouls like to play?
Corpse and robbers.

What is a ghost's favourite music?
Haunting melodies.

Did you hear about the champagne party?
It was a real corker.

Why is Frankenstein such good fun at parties?
He'll have you in stitches.

What did Paul Daniels say at the Christmas party?
'How's tricks?'

Did you hear about Dracula's Christmas party?
It was a scream.

Did you hear about the party with lots of fireworks and crackers and balloons?
It went with a bang.

What did Dracula say at the Christmas party?
'Fancy a bite?'

Why couldn't the skeleton go to the New Year's Eve ball?
He had no body to go with.

Why did the skeleton go to the party?
For a rattlin' good time.

What would you expect to see at a chicken show?
Hentertainment.

Where will you always find diamonds?
In a pack of cards.

What pipes are never played in Scotland on New Year's Eve?
Hose pipes.

Ring out the Old, Ring in the New

What is found at the end of the year?
The letter 'R'.

What did Queen Victoria say on the first day of January, 1885?
'Happy New Year.'

What does a caterpillar do on New Year's Day?
Turn over a new leaf.